CULTIVATE SACRED SOIL
STUDY GUIDE

Copyright © 2025 by Josh Weisbrod

Published by Arrows and Stones

All rights reserved. No portion of this book may be reproduced, stored in a retrieval system, or transmitted in any form or by any means—electronic, mechanical, photocopy, recording, scanning, or other—except for brief quotations in critical reviews or articles, without prior written permission of the author.

Unless otherwise specified, all Scripture quotations are taken from The ESV® Bible (The Holy Bible, English Standard Version®), copyright © 2001 by Crossway, a publishing ministry of Good News Publishers. Used by permission. All rights reserved. | Scripture quotations marked NIV are taken from the Holy Bible, New International Version®, NIV®. Copyright © 1973, 1978, 1984, 2011 by Biblica, Inc.™ Used by permission of Zondervan. All rights reserved worldwide. www.zondervan.com. The "NIV" and "New International Version" are trademarks registered in the United States Patent and Trademark Office by Biblica, Inc.™

For foreign and subsidiary rights, contact the author.

Cover design by Josh Weisbrod

ISBN: 978-1-964794-21-1   1 2 3 4 5 6 7 8 9 10

Printed in the United States of America

CULTIVATE SACRED SOIL

STUDY GUIDE

JOSHUA WEISBROD

CONTENTS

Introduction 6

CH 1. **CHANGING THE METAPHOR** 10

CH 2. **THE LIFE GOD CREATED YOU FOR** 16

CH 3. **START DIGGING** 22

CH 4. **TRUE REST** 28

CH 5. **FOLLOW THE LEADER** 34

CH 6. **AWESOME SPLENDOR** 40

CH 7. **LIFT YOUR EYES** 46

CH 8. **THE RESTORATION OF PRAYER** 52

CH 9. **FROM OVERGROWN TO OPEN** 60

CH 10. **COMMUNITY INCREASES GROWTH** 66

CH 11. **THE WONDERFUL, MESSY WORK OF PEOPLE** . . 72

CH 12. **GET YOUR HANDS DIRTY** 78

CULTIVATE
SACRED SOIL

*Nurture the soil of your heart for
a life that thrives in Christ*

JOSHUA WEISBROD

INTRODUCTION

Cultivation isn't complicated,
but it is multi-faceted.

READING TIME

As you read the Introduction in *Cultivate Sacred Soil*, review, reflect on, and respond to the text by answering the following questions.

REVIEW, REFLECT, AND RESPOND

Reflect on your current relationship with God. If your spiritual life were a garden, how would you describe its condition?

_____
_____
_____
_____
_____
_____
_____

How comfortable are you with allowing God to disrupt your comfort zones for the sake of growth?

_____
_____
_____
_____
_____
_____
_____
_____
_____

Cultivating sacred soil requires both effort and surrender. How do you balance working diligently to grow your faith while trusting God to work according to his will? How might the Holy Spirit be inviting you to adjust this balance in your current season?

_____
_____
_____
_____
_____
_____
_____
_____
_____
_____

Think about a time when you tried to rush a spiritual breakthrough or resolution. What did you learn about God's timing and your role in the process?

_____
_____
_____
_____
_____
_____
_____
_____
_____
_____

Reflect on the purpose of this book: to cultivate sacred soil in your heart. What specific changes or breakthroughs are you hoping to see in your spiritual life as you work through this book?

_____
_____
_____
_____
_____
_____
_____
_____
_____
_____
_____

CHAPTER 1

CHANGING THE METAPHOR

CULTIVATION IS NOT SIMPLY ABOUT WHAT WE DO BUT HOW WE DO IT.

READING TIME

As you read Chapter 1: "Changing the Metaphor" in *Cultivate Sacred Soil*, review, reflect on, and respond to the text by answering the following questions.

REVIEW, REFLECT, AND RESPOND

Which aspect of the metaphor of tending a garden as a way to cultivate a deep relationship with Christ resonates with you the most, and why?

_____
_____
_____
_____
_____
_____

How does the tendency for Christians to "reset" their faith after failures resonate with your own faith walk? How can you reframe your thinking to embrace growth in Christ as a process rather than a pass-fail system?

_____
_____
_____
_____
_____
_____

What areas of your faith journey feel "uncultivated" right now, and how might this relate to resistance to growth or impatience with the process of spiritual maturity?

_____
_____
_____
_____
_____

> **"I have been crucified with Christ. It is no longer I who live, but Christ who lives in me. And the life I now live in the flesh I live by faith in the Son of God, who loved me and gave himself for me."**
> **—Galatians 2:20**

Consider the scripture above and answer the following questions:

Reflect on the phrase "Christ who lives in me." How do you see evidence of Christ's life within you today?

_____
_____
_____
_____
_____

Consider how you handle setbacks and failures. In what ways do your current patterns reflect Christ's presence within you, and where do you see room for growth in embodying this truth?

_____
_____

In what ways do you see the need for pruning (removing unproductive habits or sins) in your spiritual life? If you aren't sure, ask the Holy Spirit to reveal those areas to you. How might you be resisting the pruning process?

It is important to nurture, prune, and be patient with the cultivation process. Which of these feels most relevant to your faith walk right now, and why?

How would you describe, in your own words, the heart posture involved in abiding in Christ?

_____
_____
_____
_____
_____
_____
_____
_____

What practices can you implement to "prepare the soil" of your heart for greater receptivity to God's Word?

_____
_____
_____
_____
_____
_____
_____
_____

Consider the role of seasons in both gardening and spiritual growth. What season do you feel you are in, and how does understanding it guide your next steps for growth?

_____
_____
_____
_____
_____
_____
_____
_____

How has this chapter either challenged your perspective or affirmed your experiences as you have worked to deepen your faith in Christ?

_____
_____
_____
_____
_____
_____
_____
_____

CHAPTER 2

THE LIFE GOD CREATED YOU FOR

THE PRESENCE OF GOD DOES HAVE A CONDITION: HE WILL NOT FORCE HIS WAY INTO A HOME THAT DOES NOT INVITE HIM.

READING TIME

As you read Chapter 2: "The Life God Created You For" in *Cultivate Sacred Soil*, review, reflect on, and respond to the text by answering the following questions.

REVIEW, REFLECT, AND RESPOND

When you reflect on your longing for closeness with a child or someone you deeply care about, how does this mirror God's desire for intimacy with you? In what ways does it shift your perspective on current circumstances or choices?

_____
_____
_____
_____
_____
_____
_____

What are your experiences with coming into the presence of God? Do you find it challenging or simple?

_____
_____
_____
_____
_____
_____
_____

In what ways are you living out the purpose God gave man since the Garden? How has He positioned you to steward what He has given you?

_____

_____

_____

_____

_____

> **"The Lord God took the man and put him in the garden of Eden to work it and keep it."**
> **—Genesis 2:15**

Consider the scripture above and answer the following questions:

How does the command to "work and keep" the garden apply to your responsibilities and relationships today?

_____

_____

_____

_____

_____

_____

_____

In what ways are you actively cultivating "the garden" that God has entrusted to you? Are there areas where you feel you've fallen short, and how can you refocus?

_____

_____

_____

In what ways is your sense of purpose connected to experiencing the presence of God?

Sin disrupts our ability to live in God's presence. What patterns in your life might be hindering your communion with God?

How does knowing that God, despite your sin and shortcomings, is actively seeking and working to become more intimate with you encourage you to prioritize His presence?

_____
_____
_____
_____
_____
_____
_____

To what extent are you inviting God into your daily life?

_____
_____
_____
_____
_____
_____
_____
_____
_____
_____

How closely does your daily belief in Christ's restoration to a life of God's presence align with your understanding of this truth?

_____
_____
_____
_____
_____
_____
_____
_____

What insights from this chapter have helped you understand God's ultimate goal for His relationship with you?

_____
_____
_____
_____
_____
_____
_____
_____

CHAPTER 3

START DIGGING

Worship is not rooted first in singing; it is founded in the heart.

READING TIME

As you read Chapter 3: "Start Digging" in *Cultivate Sacred Soil*, review, reflect on, and respond to the text by answering the following questions.

REVIEW, REFLECT, AND RESPOND

Recall a time when you felt yourself being led by the Holy Spirit. In what ways did your flesh war against you? What does it look like to submit your flesh to the Spirit?

_____
_____
_____
_____
_____
_____
_____

What voices do you wrestle with that attempt to deprive you of community and other activities that are vital for cultivating your faith?

_____
_____
_____
_____
_____
_____
_____

What does it mean to cultivate holiness in your life, and how might you be exhausting yourself by trying to "activate" it rather than cultivate it (allowing it to grow through intentional effort and surrender)?

___

> **"But the fruit of the Spirit is love, joy, peace, forbearance, kindness, goodness, faithfulness, gentleness and self-control. Against such things, there is no law. Those who belong to Christ Jesus have crucified the flesh with its passions and desires. Since we live by the Spirit, let us keep in step with the Spirit."**
> **—Galatians 5:22-25 (NIV)**

Consider the scripture above and answer the following questions:

The fruit of the Spirit encompasses many characteristics. Which one is the hardest for you to embody in your current season, and what does this reveal about areas of your heart that may need deeper cultivation?

___

How do you recognize when you are living "in step with the Spirit" versus following your own desires? What practical habits help you stay aligned with the Spirit in your daily walk?

_____
_____
_____
_____
_____

How deeply do you engage with Scripture—not just reading, but allowing it to transform you? What specific part of Scripture could you begin reading in small, bite-size portions, and how might you invite the Holy Spirit to guide and illuminate your understanding as you engage with it?

_____
_____
_____
_____
_____

Consider areas of your life where you might be tolerating sin. What would it take from you to finally win the battle over your flesh in this area?

_____
_____
_____
_____
_____

Worship is described as offering God your whole heart. What parts of your heart are you withholding from God, and why? Ask the Holy Spirit to reveal the fears underlying that resistance. How might submitting those things to Him be an act of worship?

_____
_____
_____
_____
_____
_____
_____
_____

How can you approach your daily responsibilities—work, relationships, rest—as acts of worship that glorify God?

_____
_____
_____
_____
_____
_____
_____
_____

Spiritual growth is a process that requires patience. How do you handle seasons of waiting in your faith, and what might God be teaching you in those times?

_____
_____
_____
_____
_____
_____
_____
_____

Reflect on how you prioritize time to cultivate your relationship with God. What does your current schedule reveal about what you truly value, and what adjustments might be needed?

_____
_____
_____
_____
_____
_____
_____
_____

CHAPTER 4

TRUE REST

The modern world does not prioritize or even appreciate healthy modes of rest.

READING TIME

As you read Chapter 4: "True Rest" in *Cultivate Sacred Soil*, review, reflect on, and respond to the text by answering the following questions.

REVIEW, REFLECT, AND RESPOND

The chapter discusses how modern culture often misunderstands or neglects rest. How do your current habits reflect society's view of busyness versus God's design for rest?

_____
_____
_____
_____
_____
_____
_____

Reflect on the concept of God's rest as dwelling in the glory of His creation. How often do you pause to truly acknowledge and celebrate God's work in your life? What might be preventing you from doing so?

_____
_____
_____
_____
_____
_____
_____

Why does God consider rest to be an intentional and active practice rather than simply a state of inactivity?

_____
_____
_____
_____
_____

> **"Thus the heavens and the earth were finished, and all the host of them. And on the seventh day God finished his work that he had done, and he rested on the seventh day from all his work that he had done. So God blessed the seventh day and made it holy, because on it God rested from all his work that he had done in creation."**
> **—Galatians 2:1-3**

Consider the scripture above and answer the following questions:

God rested not because He needed to but to reflect and declare His creation as "good." How often do you take time to pause and reflect on God's goodness in your life?

_____
_____
_____
_____
_____

When you take time to rest, how do you usually spend it, and how do your choices during that time impact your relationship with God—do they draw you closer to Him or create distance?

_____
_____
_____
_____
_____
_____

The chapter describes rest as a divine gift. In what ways are you receiving or rejecting this gift in your current life?

_____
_____
_____
_____
_____
_____

God rested to dwell in the glory of His creation, yet many of us struggle to dwell in His presence. What distractions or beliefs keep you from fully embracing the rest God offers?

_____
_____
_____
_____
_____
_____

The chapter contrasts worldly rest with true rest in God. How does your current approach to rest reflect worldly priorities, and how can you shift toward God-centered rest?

_____
_____
_____
_____
_____
_____
_____
_____

Rest is connected to trust in God. How does this resonate with you as you consider your relationship with God?

_____
_____
_____
_____
_____
_____
_____
_____

In a culture that idolizes busyness, how can you model God's rest to others? What might this testimony of rest say about your trust in Him?

_____
_____
_____
_____
_____
_____
_____

What does it mean to rest in Jesus and be yoked with Him?

_____
_____
_____
_____
_____
_____
_____
_____
_____
_____

CHAPTER 5

FOLLOW THE LEADER

IF JESUS FULFILLED HIS CALLING AND
FOUND REST, YOU CAN TOO.

READING TIME

As you read Chapter 5: "Follow the Leader" in *Cultivate Sacred Soil*, review, reflect on, and respond to the text by answering the following questions.

REVIEW, REFLECT, AND RESPOND

When have you learned by observing another person?

_____
_____
_____
_____
_____
_____
_____
_____

What insights about following Christ's leadership can you gain by observing how He related to His disciples?

_____
_____
_____
_____
_____
_____
_____
_____

In what areas of your life do you feel anxious due to unrealistic expectations—whether self-imposed or from others —about what it means to live a faithful Christian life?

___

Following a leader requires humility. In what areas of your life might pride or self-reliance be preventing you from fully surrendering to God's guidance?

___

> **"And he said to them, 'Come away by yourselves to a desolate place and rest a while.' For many were coming and going, and they had no leisure even to eat."**
> **—Mark 6:31**

Consider the scripture above and answer the following questions:

Jesus invited His disciples to step away and rest after their mission. How do you find yourself resisting His command to rest, even when you believe the work you are doing is part of the mission He has called you to?

___

How does this scripture emphasize the significance of listening to God's leading to rest, even when there are essential tasks that still need attention?

Consider the statement, "No part of our faith is a solo expedition." In what ways have you been trying to walk alone, and how can you lean into community and discipleship instead?

What reasons or justifications do you often use to avoid resting, even when you sense God is calling you to it?

What kind of boundaries have you established in your life, and how well do you enforce them? How often do you feel overwhelmed in your relationships, and what does that reveal about the boundaries you have in place?

_____
_____
_____
_____
_____
_____

How has your understanding of rest and purpose evolved after reading about how Jesus models balance? Where do you see this need for balance in your current life?

_____
_____
_____
_____
_____
_____
_____

If someone new to faith were looking at your life as an example, what would they learn? Would they see a reflection of Christ in your actions, and what could you improve to make that reflection clearer?

_____
_____
_____
_____
_____
_____
_____
_____

What does your current daily rhythm of rest look like, and what changes could you make to strengthen or establish it more intentionally?

_____
_____
_____
_____
_____
_____
_____
_____

CHAPTER 6

AWESOME SPLENDOR

Wherever you are right now, you can experience the awe of His glory.

READING TIME

As you read Chapter 6: "Awesome Splendor" in *Cultivate Sacred Soil*, review, reflect on, and respond to the text by answering the following questions.

REVIEW, REFLECT, AND RESPOND

When was the last time you were truly in awe of something? When was the last time you were in awe of God? How did those moments impact you, and how do they differ from simply experiencing something exciting or impressive?

_____
_____
_____
_____
_____
_____

What is the difference between being afraid of God and the fear of the Lord? Consider the listed scriptures in this chapter that speak of the fear of the Lord. Which of these resonates with you the most, and why? Which challenges you the most?

_____
_____
_____
_____
_____
_____

Why should the cultivation of awe always point us back to Jesus?

___

> "Where can I go from your Spirit? Where can I flee from your presence? If I go up to the heavens, you are there; if I make my bed in the depths, you are there. If I rise on the wings of the dawn, if I settle on the far side of the sea, even there your hand will guide me, your right hand will hold me fast."
> —Psalm 139:7-10 (NIV)

Consider the scripture above and answer the following questions:

The idea that God's hand guides and holds you no matter where you are reflects His omnipotence and care. How does this truth deepen your wonder at His ability to personally engage with every aspect of your life?

Why is God's inescapable presence—in everything we do, say, and think—something to be revered and cherished rather than feared?

_____
_____
_____
_____
_____
_____

Awe is more than a fleeting feeling but a posture of heart. Are you postured to cultivate a life of awe? How can you cultivate a lasting sense of awe in your daily walk with Christ?

_____
_____
_____
_____
_____
_____

Why do you think it can be so difficult and feel unnatural to cultivate a life of awe?

_____
_____
_____
_____
_____
_____

The chapter emphasizes that the awe of God leads to transformation. Why do you think awe is necessary in order to be transformed into His image?

_____
_____
_____
_____
_____
_____
_____

How does worship of God's creation pervert the true worship our lives were meant to offer?

_____
_____
_____
_____
_____
_____
_____

Take a moment in quiet solitude to reflect on the awe of the cross. What kind of images, thoughts, and emotions came up for you, and what did the Holy Spirit reveal to you?

_____
_____
_____
_____
_____
_____
_____

What experiences do you have with transactional worship? In what ways might focusing on what you can "get" from worship hinder your ability to fully experience God's presence?

_____
_____
_____
_____
_____
_____
_____
_____

CHAPTER 7

LIFT YOUR EYES

God has not asked you to bear the weight of the world. He has called you to find your rest and security in Him.

READING TIME

As you read Chapter 7: "Lift Your Eyes" in *Cultivate Sacred Soil*, review, reflect on, and respond to the text by answering the following questions.

REVIEW, REFLECT, AND RESPOND

How does the way we view our troubles dictate their size? Consider today's troubles. Have you made them into mountains? Have you taken time to stand in awe of God?

_____
_____
_____
_____
_____
_____

Psalm 63 displays the joy and peace of God we can feel even in the midst of defeat and weariness. Read through the psalm. What word, phrase, or line jumped out to you, and why? How does it apply to your life?

_____
_____
_____
_____
_____
_____

Who in your life lives in awe of God, and how often do you surround yourself with those people? What about them sets them apart?

_____
_____
_____
_____
_____
_____
_____
_____

> **"I lift up my eyes to the hills. From where does my help come? My help comes from the LORD, who made heaven and earth."**
> **—Psalm 121:1-2**

Consider the scripture above and answer the following questions:

How easy is it for you to "lift up your eyes," and how might the time you've spent cultivating awe be linked to that?

_____
_____
_____
_____
_____
_____
_____
_____

Recall a time when you sought help outside of God. What was that experience like, and what was the result? What have you learned from it?

_____
_____
_____
_____
_____
_____
_____
_____
_____

How is the awe of God evident in your life in the context of ministry? What aspects of Christ's goodness are you actively sharing with the world?

_____
_____
_____
_____
_____
_____
_____
_____
_____
_____
_____

How do you keep your eyes on the work of Christ here on earth and the hope of eternity simultaneously? How does getting a glimpse of heaven now prepare us for a life of eternal glory in the future?

_____
_____
_____
_____
_____
_____
_____

Where on the spectrum of standing in awe of God and religious participation do you fall right now? What habits or beliefs do you need to leave behind in order to trade the latter for the former?

_____
_____
_____
_____
_____
_____
_____
_____

Do you tend to approach God in prayer with a "laundry list" of requests? How has this approach to God detracted from a rich, abiding relationship with Him? In what spaces of your life could you begin to cultivate the awe of God?

_____
_____
_____
_____
_____
_____
_____

CHAPTER 8

THE RESTORATION OF PRAYER

THERE WILL ALWAYS BE A LOSS OF INTIMACY WHEN WE SHIFT PRAYER FROM BEING ABOUT JESUS TO BEING ABOUT US.

READING TIME

As you read Chapter 8: "The Restoration of Prayer" in *Cultivate Sacred Soil*, review, reflect on, and respond to the text by answering the following questions.

REVIEW, REFLECT, AND RESPOND

How would you describe your current prayer life? In what ways do you experience the duality of prayer that the disciples of Christ experienced?

_____
_____
_____
_____
_____
_____
_____

What do you notice about the model of how to pray that Jesus gave His disciples? How does this model differ from the way many Christians approach prayer?

_____
_____
_____
_____
_____
_____
_____

What role does listening play in your prayer life?

_____
_____
_____
_____
_____
_____

> **"Come near to God, and he will come near to you. Wash your hands, you sinners, and purify your hearts, you double-minded. Grieve, mourn and wail. Change your laughter to mourning and your joy to gloom. Humble yourselves before the Lord, and he will lift you up."**
> **—James 4:8-10 (NIV)**

Consider the scripture above and answer the following questions:

According to this passage, we are to draw near first. Why do you think God waits for us to draw near to Him?

_____
_____
_____
_____
_____
_____
_____

Why does James urge us to grieve, mourn, and wail, asking us to turn laughter into mourning and joy into gloom? How can this be understood as an invitation to deeper intimacy with God rather than a negative command to embrace sadness?

_____
_____
_____
_____
_____
_____
_____

Meditate on who God says He is, and craft your own personal prayer using the ACTS model as a general framework:

Adoration: _____

_____
_____
_____
_____
_____

Confession: _____

_____
_____
_____
_____
_____

Thanksgiving: _____

_____

_____

_____

_____

_____

Supplication: _____

_____

_____

_____

_____

_____

Have you ever doubted that God is listening to your prayers? Where does the doubt come from, and why can you have confidence that silence is not negligence?

_____

_____

_____

_____

_____

What are some different ways God has answered your prayers in the past? Share a time when God answered quickly and another when you had to wait. What lessons from those experiences can help you trust Him as you wait now?

How consistent are you in your prayer life? What would it look like to "pray constantly"? What do you think Paul meant by that in 1 Thessalonians 5:17?

_____

_____

_____

_____

_____

_____

_____

_____

Are your prayers more focused on you or on Jesus? How does a Jesus-centered prayer life look different than a self-centered prayer life?

_____

_____

_____

_____

_____

_____

_____

_____

How did this chapter challenge the way you pray? How can you realign your heart to pray with faith, fully trusting in who God declares Himself to be?

_____
_____
_____
_____
_____
_____
_____

CHAPTER 9

FROM OVERGROWN TO OPEN

It's not about what God will do but what we allow Him to do in our lives.

READING TIME

As you read Chapter 9: "From Overgrown to Open" in *Cultivate Sacred Soil*, review, reflect on, and respond to the text by answering the following questions.

REVIEW, REFLECT, AND RESPOND

What overgrown areas of your life might be creating a sense of distance between you and God?

_____
_____
_____
_____
_____
_____
_____

How has the presence of "good things" like work, family, or ministry unintentionally undermined your prayer life?

_____
_____
_____
_____
_____
_____
_____

What is your experience with the pruning process? What do you think would happen if God didn't cut away the branches that do not bear fruit?

> "I am the true vine, and my Father is the vinedresser. Every branch in me that does not bear fruit he takes away, and every branch that does bear fruit he prunes, that it may bear more fruit."
> —John 15:1-2

Consider the scripture above and answer the following questions:

According to this scripture, pruning involves cutting away parts of the plant. What areas of your life might God be pruning right now, and how can you respond with trust and obedience?

What fruits do you see emerging in your life as a result of God's careful pruning?

How did you initially react to the idea that God has already spoken the "first word" and, in prayer, we respond with the "second word"? How does this principle align with or differ from the way you currently approach your prayer life?

Reflect on a time when you allowed the Holy Spirit to lead your prayers. How did that experience differ from times when you relied solely on your own thoughts or words? In what ways does His intercession free us?

Praying in the name of Jesus means aligning with His will. How do you ensure that your requests in prayer reflect the character and purposes of Christ rather than personal desires? How could you apply this right now to a specific prayer you are currently lifting up?

_____
_____
_____
_____
_____
_____

Think of a recent prayer where you struggled to find the right words. What scripture might have helped you articulate your heart and align your request with God's promises?

_____
_____
_____
_____
_____
_____
_____

What are the risks of basing your faith on your emotions or the feeling of intimacy with Christ instead of grounding it in Christ Himself?

_____
_____
_____
_____
_____
_____
_____

How would you describe the current state of your prayer life? Overgrown? Well-tended? Thriving? What work is needed?

_____
_____
_____
_____
_____
_____
_____

CHAPTER 10

COMMUNITY INCREASES GROWTH

Your value in the Kingdom isn't determined by worldly value; it's set in stone by God.

READING TIME

As you read Chapter 10: "Community Increases Growth" in *Cultivate Sacred Soil*, review, reflect on, and respond to the text by answering the following questions.

REVIEW, REFLECT, AND RESPOND

Reflect on an area of your life where you've operated in isolation rather than community. How has this impacted your ability to cultivate your faith?

_____
_____
_____
_____
_____
_____

Who in your community has played a role in helping you thrive spiritually, and how can you actively pour into them?

_____
_____
_____
_____
_____
_____
_____

How willing are you to make sacrifices for your relationships (e.g., laying down your busy schedule), and how well do you do that in your closest relationships now?

___

> "May the God who gives endurance and encouragement give you the same attitude of mind toward each other that Christ Jesus had, so that with one mind and one voice you may glorify the God and Father of our Lord Jesus Christ."
> —Romans 15:5-6 (NIV)

Consider the scripture above and answer the following questions:

This scripture encourages unity in glorifying God. How does your attitude toward others in your community reflect or hinder this unity?

___

How can you cultivate a "one mind and one voice" mentality with those around you to better glorify God?

_____
_____
_____
_____
_____

How do you balance independence with the humility to rely on others for support and encouragement?

_____
_____
_____
_____
_____

In what ways has the artificial communal landscape of the Westernized modern world eclipsed opportunities for authentic, participatory relationships with others?

_____
_____
_____
_____
_____

How have you struggled to forgive someone within your community or circle of influence, and what steps can you take to usher in forgiveness?

_____
_____
_____
_____
_____
_____
_____

How do you see your unique gifts contributing to the larger community, and are there ways you've been holding back?

_____
_____
_____
_____
_____
_____
_____
_____

In what ways did Jesus embrace the "messiness" of people and relationships, and how could you approach your messiest relationships as Jesus did?

_____
_____
_____
_____
_____
_____
_____

How can you more actively treat community-building as an act of worship, not just a social obligation?

_____
_____
_____
_____
_____
_____
_____
_____

CHAPTER 11

THE WONDERFUL, MESSY WORK OF PEOPLE

THE EXTENSION OF GRACE TO OTHERS MUST BE A REGULAR RHYTHM OF OUR LIVES, NOT SEVEN TIMES, BUT CONTINUOUSLY.

READING TIME

As you read Chapter 11: "The Wonderful, Messy Work of People" in *Cultivate Sacred Soil*, review, reflect on, and respond to the text by answering the following questions.

REVIEW, REFLECT, AND RESPOND

Reflect on a recent situation where relational challenges either softened or hardened your spirit. What did you learn from that experience?

_____
_____
_____
_____
_____
_____
_____

How do you currently respond to the "thorns" in your relationships, and how might God be using them to shape your character?

_____
_____
_____
_____
_____
_____
_____

Do you often allow the fear of betrayal or pain to deter you from forging deep relationships with people? Why is the risk of getting hurt worth the effort and courage to continue pursuing and serving people in faith?

_____
_____
_____
_____

> **"Bear with each other and forgive one another if any of you has a grievance against someone. Forgive as the Lord forgave you."**
> **—Colossians 3:13 (NIV)**

Consider the scripture above and answer the following questions:

How readily are you able to forgive others? How might it become an obstacle to cultivating deep intimacy with God?

_____
_____
_____
_____
_____
_____
_____
_____

Forgiveness is a command, not an option. What grievances are you currently holding onto, and how might releasing them bring freedom and deeper alignment with Christ's example?

___

Reflecting on the advice to "let it go" when people leave messily, how do you currently handle unresolved relational wounds, and what might God be calling you to release?

___

Why do you think Jesus calls us to unlimited forgiveness? How does that command challenge you?

_____
_____
_____
_____
_____
_____
_____
_____

Why is messiness a beautiful thing rather than a burdensome thing or something to be avoided?

_____
_____
_____
_____
_____
_____
_____
_____

Do you place unrealistic expectations on people to love you better than you are able to love? How does recognizing your own imperfections strengthen your relationship with Christ and help you grow in loving others more authentically?

_____
_____
_____
_____
_____
_____
_____

In what ways do you encourage and edify others? Who could you encourage today?

_____
_____
_____
_____
_____
_____
_____
_____

CHAPTER 12

GET YOUR HANDS DIRTY

The most important part of cultivating your faith is looking at Jesus, God's Son.

READING TIME

As you read Chapter 12: "Get Your Hands Dirty" in *Cultivate Sacred Soil*, review, reflect on, and respond to the text by answering the following questions.

REVIEW, REFLECT, AND RESPOND

Reflect on a recent failure in your spiritual journey. How did you respond to it?

_____
_____
_____
_____
_____
_____
_____

How does the fear of failure affect your willingness to step out in faith, and how can you reframe failure as part of the growth process?

_____
_____
_____
_____
_____
_____
_____

How has your response to failure evolved over the course of your walk with Christ? To what degree does it reflect the reception of God's grace as we are purified and sanctified?

_____
_____
_____
_____
_____
_____
_____
_____
_____
_____

What is one small, specific action you can take this week to cultivate your faith or serve others more intentionally?

_____
_____
_____
_____
_____
_____
_____
_____
_____
_____
_____
_____
_____

How are the processes of failure and learning part of good stewardship?

_____

_____

_____

_____

_____

_____

_____

_____

_____

Reflect on the past few years of your life. In what ways have you grown? What do you know now that you didn't know then, and what does that tell you about the power of intentional, gradual cultivation?

_____

_____

_____

_____

_____

_____

_____

_____

_____

_____

Where is Jesus leading you now? In what areas of your life do you feel God is calling you to focus on cultivating growth?

_____
_____
_____
_____
_____
_____
_____

What small step can you take to gain momentum in cultivating your faith and relationship with Christ?

_____
_____
_____
_____
_____
_____
_____
_____
_____

How does self-criticism tend to show up in your faith walk? List three wins that you can celebrate right now.

_____

_____

_____

_____

_____

_____

_____

What did you learn from this book, and in what ways will you begin to apply those principles to your life?

_____

_____

_____

_____

_____

_____

_____

www.ingramcontent.com/pod-product-compliance
Lightning Source LLC
Chambersburg PA
CBHW062120080426
42734CB00012B/2926